Donated by
Editorial Directions
in honor of
The Koutris Family
to the
Olive-Mary Stitt LMC
Fall 2005

CHLORINE

CHLORINE
UN1017
INHALATION HAZARD

A TRUE BOOK®

by
Salvatore Tocci

Children's Press®
A Division of Scholastic Inc.

New York Toronto London Auckland Sydney
Mexico City New Delhi Hong Kong
Danbury, Connecticut

Chlorine is used to make jogging shoes.

Reading Consultant
Julia McKenzie Munemo, MEd
New York, New York

Science Consultant
John A. Benner
Austin, Texas

The photo on the cover shows chlorine tablets. The photo on the title page shows chlorine tanks.

The author and the publisher are not responsible for injuries or accidents that occur during or from any experiments. Experiments should be conducted in the presence of or with the help of an adult. Any instructions of the experiments that require the use of sharp, hot, or other unsafe items should be conducted by or with the help of an adult.

Library of Congress Cataloging-in-Publication Data

Tocci, Salvatore.
    Chlorine / by Salvatore Tocci.
        p. cm. — (A true book)
    Includes bibliographical references and index.
    ISBN 0-516-23698-9 (lib. bdg.)   0-516-25574-6 (pbk.)
    1. Chlorine—Juvenile literature. I. Title. II. Series.
QD181.C5T5 2005
546'732—dc22   2004027156

Contents

A swimming pool is many people's favorite place to swim.

Do You Like to Swim?

Where's your favorite place to go swimming? Perhaps you like swimming in the ocean because of the waves. Maybe you prefer swimming in freshwater, such as in a pond or lake. Perhaps your favorite place to swim is a swimming pool.

5

If you like to swim in a pool, then you know how important it is to keep the water clean. The water is constantly passing through a filter that traps and removes small **particles**. Larger particles that fall to the bottom of the pool are vacuumed up to keep the water clean. Removing these particles, however, is only part of keeping the water in a swimming pool clean and clear.

Anyone who takes care of a swimming pool knows how important it is to check the quality of the water. One way to test the water in a pool is to check the chlorine level. If the chlorine level is too low, a green slime may appear on the bottom and sides of the pool. If that happens, people won't even want to go in the water! But when the chlorine level is too high, the water can irritate a swimmer's eyes.

This woman is testing the level of chlorine in the swimming pool water.

Swimming isn't fun when the water makes your eyes burn and sting.

The chlorine level must be just right so that everyone can enjoy swimming in the pool. You need chlorine to keep the water in a swimming pool clean. As you will learn in this book, there are many other important uses for chlorine.

What Is Chlorine?

Chlorine is an **element**. An element is one of the building blocks of **matter**. Matter is the stuff or material that makes up everything in the universe. This book, the chair you are sitting on, and even your body are all made of matter.

There are millions of different kinds of matter. However, there are just a few more than one hundred different elements. How can so many different kinds of matter be made up of so few elements?

Think about the English language. Just twenty-six letters can be arranged to make up all the words in our language. Likewise, the one hundred elements can be arranged in countless ways to create all the different kinds of matter in the universe.

Chlorine was officially discovered by a British scientist in 1810. Actually, a Swedish scientist discovered chlorine in 1774. This scientist, however, did not realize that he had discovered a new element. The British scientist was the first to recognize that chlorine is an element and give it a name.

JUMBO CHLORINATOR TABLETS - 3"

This duck dispenser holds chlorine tablets that will help keep the pool water clean.

Turning Green

Find out why people who spend a lot of time in swimming pools notice that their hair turns a little green. Pour 6 ounces (about 190 milliliters) of swimming pool water into two cups. Use a pool water test kit to check the chlorine level of the water in one cup. Be sure not to touch the water. Then place your finger into the other cup.

Keep it in the water for at least two minutes. Take out your finger and check the chlorine level of the water. You should find that the chlorine level is lower. Your finger has absorbed some of the chlorine. People who spend a lot of time in a swimming pool can absorb enough chlorine through their bodies to turn their hair green.

15

Chlorine gets its name from the Greek word *chloros*, which means "light green." The British scientist gave chlorine its name because the substance he had discovered was a greenish yellow gas.

Every element has a name and a symbol made up of one, two, or three letters. The symbol for chlorine is Cl.

At room temperature, chlorine is a greenish yellow gas that is heavier than air.

Chlorine gas is a dangerous substance. Its powerful smell can cause a person to choke. Anyone who inhales even a small amount of chlorine gas may feel a tightness in the throat. If more chlorine gas is inhaled, a person's lungs can start to fill with fluid.

Because of its effects on people, chlorine became the first gas used in chemical warfare. During World War I, the Germans fired artillery shells at

French troops defending a position in northern France. The shells were filled with chlorine gas. When they exploded, the shells released chlorine gas, which slowly drifted to the ground. The gas filled the trenches in which the French soldiers were protecting themselves. After inhaling the chlorine, the French soldiers became ill and fainted. Many died.

Chlorine was the first poison gas used in warfare.

The amount of chlorine added to swimming pool and drinking water is enough to kill green slime and bacteria but not enough to harm a person.

Liquid chlorine is also very dangerous. Chlorine gas can easily be turned into a liquid by cooling it. Liquid chlorine burns the skin.

Although liquid chlorine can be harmful, it can also be useful. In the early 1900s, liquid chlorine was added to drinking water supplies in the United States to kill germs. At the time, some people were dying from diseases caused by certain germs in their drinking water.

In 1900, just one of these diseases alone killed about 25,000 Americans.

Once liquid chlorine was added to drinking water supplies, many diseases no longer posed a serious threat. By the 1920s, chlorine gas had replaced chlorine liquid for treating drinking water.

Unfortunately, people in many developing regions of the world still drink water that has not been treated with chlorine.

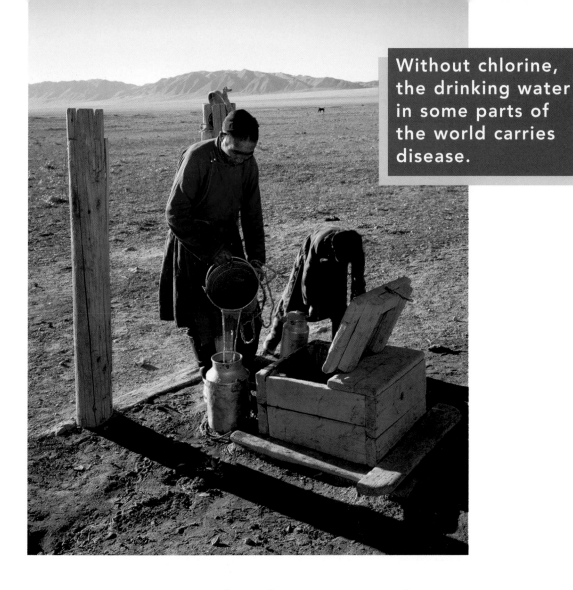

Without chlorine, the drinking water in some parts of the world carries disease.

As a result, these people are still exposed to outbreaks of deadly diseases.

Why Is Chlorine Not Found Alone?

Chlorine seldom exists as an element in nature. It is usually found as part of a **compound**. A compound is made of two or more different elements that are combined into a single substance. Chlorine is rarely found by itself in nature because it is very active. This means that chlorine combines very quickly and easily with other elements to form a compound. Many chlorine compounds are very useful.

One example of a useful chlorine compound is laundry bleach. If you check the label on a container of bleach, you will probably see the words *sodium hypochlorite*. This is

Bleach is a chlorine compound.

the name of the compound that contains chlorine.

Laundry bleach is used to remove stains on clothing. A colored stain is actually a compound. The compound is made up of a long string of elements that are attached to one another, like beads on a string. Bleach works by breaking this long compound into smaller ones. These new smaller compounds are colorless.

Getting Rid of the Color

Use chlorine bleach to perform a magic trick. Ask an adult for help. Fill two clear plastic 8-ounce (250-milliliter) cups with warm water. Add a drop of red food coloring to one cup. Add four droppers full of bleach to the other cup. Tell your audience that you are about to perform some magic.

28

Pour the red liquid into the clear liquid. In less than a minute, the red solution should turn colorless. If not, experiment by adjusting the amount of bleach you add. Explain to your audience that the clear solution contained bleach that broke apart the compound responsible for the red color.

Another useful chlorine compound is hydrogen chloride. As you may be able to tell from its name, this compound is made of two elements—hydrogen and chlorine. When water is added to this compound, hydrogen chloride turns into hydrochloric acid. This acid is found in our stomachs, where it helps digest foods.

Hydrochloric acid is also used to make gelatin. The gelatin is then used to make

A chlorine compound is part of the process that is used to make all of these food products.

desserts, thicken jellies and yogurts, and make capsules for vitamin tablets.

Most homes contain another useful chlorine com- pound. This compound is sodium chloride, or table salt. Many people use sodi- um chloride to season their food. Sodium chloride is also used to soften water and to keep fish fresh. In fact, the main use of salt at one time was to preserve foods, especially meats and vegetables. This use of salt kept people's food from spoiling.

The ancient Romans valued salt so much that they often paid their soldiers with it. Using salt to pay people for their services is how the word *salary* originated.

How Has Chlorine Affected the Environment?

Some chlorine compounds have caused problems and raised concerns. One example is a group of chlorine compounds known as CFCs. These compounds were once used

34

as coolants in refrigerators and air conditioners. Scientists discovered that CFCs were slowly collecting in the atmosphere above Earth. The energy from sunlight broke apart these compounds, releasing chlorine gas. In the atmosphere, the chlorine gas started to destroy the **ozone layer**. This layer of ozone gas protects us from the harmful rays of the sun.

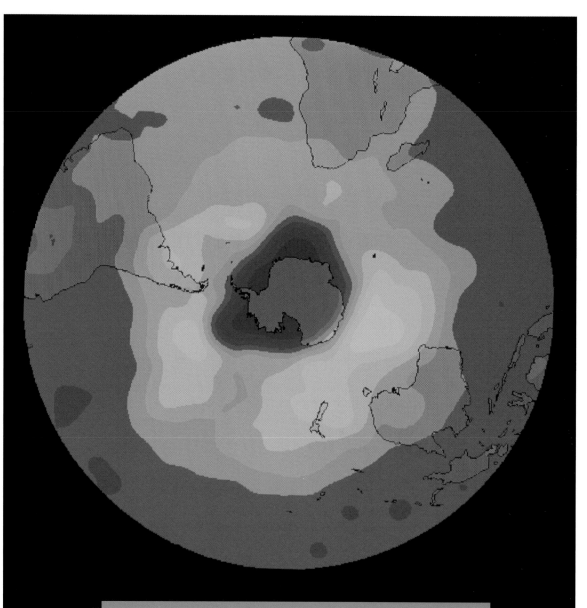

The dark blue area represents the hole in the ozone layer over Antarctica.

To stop chlorine from destroying the ozone layer, 163 nations signed an agreement in 1987. They agreed that all countries would stop using CFCs by 2010. Unfortunately, chlorine from CFCs that is already in the atmosphere continues to destroy the ozone layer.

Another chlorine compound has raised concerns about the environment. This compound is known as PVC, which is a plastic material. PVC is mainly used for construction materials, especially pipes in plumbing and irrigation systems. PVC is resistant to **corrosion** and rusting. As a result, PVC pipes may last for one hundred years or more.

PVC is also used to make a variety of medical products, such as surgical gloves, oxygen tents, and hospital mattress covers. PVC, however, is a source of concern. When PVC

These irrigation pipes contain PVC.

is burned, a toxic substance known as dioxin is released into the air. For example, dioxin is released when medical products that contain PVC are burned after they can no longer be used.

Dioxin can be carried by the wind for thousands of miles before settling to the ground. Grazing animals and fish eat the dioxin with their food. The dioxin is passed on to humans that eat these animals.

Dioxin has been shown to cause a variety of diseases, including cancer. Some people suggest that we stop using PVC and other products that contain chlorine. Others argue that the benefits outweigh the risks. They believe that we should keep using these products because chlorine provides so many benefits that make our lives healthy and more enjoyable.

Fun Facts About Chlorine

- Chlorine is the twentieth most common element on Earth. It makes up only 0.013 percent of the Earth's crust, but almost 2 percent of seawater.

- Chlorine was first used to treat drinking water in 1850 during a cholera outbreak in London, England.

- In 1847, a chlorine compound called chloroform was first used to put people to sleep during surgical operations.

- Chlorine compounds are used in the manufacture of about 10,000 consumer products, including jogging shoes, telephones, notebook paper, automobile paint, and bullet-resistant glass.

- After the two elements that make up water (hydrogen and oxygen), chlorine is the next most plentiful element in seawater.

- Scientists are exploring ways to combine chlorine with cotton fabrics so that clothes do not have to be washed as often.

To Find Out More

To find out more about chlorine, check out these additional resources.

 **Books**

Blashfield, Jean F. **Chlorine.** Raintree/Steck Vaughn, 2002.

Tocci, Salvatore. **The Periodic Table.** Children's Press, 2004.

Watt, Susan. **Chlorine.** Benchmark Books, 2001.

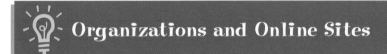

Organizations and Online Sites

U.S. Environmental Protection Agency
http://www.epa.gov/ kidshometour/products/ bleach.htm

Learn more about bleach and why it is called an antimicrobial pesticide. Find out why you should never mix chlorine bleach with any other household cleaner, especially ammonia.

The Global Bug Conspiracy
http://science-education. org/bugconspiracy/

Find out more about water-borne illnesses and how chlorine helps fight them.

Swimming Pool Germs Busted by Chlorine!
http://www.science-education.org/classroom _activities/pool.pdf

Print out an activity and coloring book about how chlorine helps keep swimming pools free of germs.

Important Words

compound substance formed when two or more different elements combine

corrosion process of wearing away slowly over time

element building block of matter

matter stuff or material that makes up everything in the universe

ozone layer layer of gas in the upper atmosphere that protects us from the sun's damaging rays

particle very tiny bit of something

Index

Meet the Author

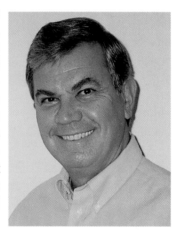

Salvatore Tocci is a science writer who lives in East Hampton, New York, with his wife, Patti. He was a high school biology and chemistry teacher for almost thirty years. His books include a high school chemistry textbook and an elementary school book series that encourages students to perform experiments to learn about science. He checks the chlorine level in his family's swimming pool at least once a week.